SMILE-A-WHILE
KNOCK KNOCKS

By Gary Chmielewski
Drawings by Ron G. Clark

© 1986 Rourke Enterprises, Inc.

All rights reserved. No part of this book may be reproduced or utilized in any form or by any means, electronic or mechanical including photocopying, recording or by any information storage and retrieval system without permission in writing from the publisher.

Library of Congress Cataloging in Publication Data

Chmielewski, Gary, 1946-
  Knock-knocks.

  (Smile-a-while joke book)
  Summary: A collection of knock-knock jokes, including "Knock, knock. Who's there? Amos. Amos who? A mosquito bit me."
  1. Knock-knock jokes. 2. Wit and humor, Juvenile.
[1. Knock-knock jokes. 2. Jokes] I. Title. II. Series.
PN6231.K55C4   1986   818'.5402   86-17780
ISBN 0-86592-684-0

ROURKE ENTERPRISES, INC.
VERO BEACH, FLORIDA 32964

Knock, Knock
Who's there?
Morris
Morris who?
Morris in the pot, so help yourself.

Knock, Knock
Who's there?
Olive
Olive who?
Olive a parade!

Knock, Knock
Who's there
Celia
Celia who?
Celia later, alligator.

Knock, Knock
Who's there?
Howie
Howie who?
Howie doing with these Knock-Knock Jokes?

Knock, Knock
Who's there?
Myra
Myra who?
Myra frigerator needs defrosting.

Knock, Knock
Who's there?
Wanda
Wanda who?
Wanda have a little fun tonight?

Knock, Knock
Who's there?
Letter
Letter who?
Letter in. It's cold outside!

Knock, Knock
Who's there?
Knecklace
Knecklace who?
Knecklace people don't get sore throats.

Knock, Knock
Who's there?
Jose
Jose who?
"Jose can you see by the dawn's early light?"

Knock, Knock
Who's there?
Cargo
Cargo who?
Cargo beep-beep!

Knock, Knock
Who's there?
Freeze
Freeze who?
Freeze a jolly good fellow.

Knock, Knock
Who's there?
Amos
Amos who?
A mosquito bit me.

Knock, Knock
Who's there?
Andy
Andy who?
And he bit me again.

Knock, Knock
Who's there?
Esther
Esther who?
Esther a bug in your soup?

Knock, Knock
Who's there?
Hair
Hair who?
Hair today, gone tomorrow.

Knock, Knock
Who's there?
Cantaloupe
Cantaloupe who?
Cantaloupe, I'm already married.

Knock, Knock
Who's there?
Atch
Atch who?
Gesundheit!

Knock, Knock
Who's there?
Avocado
Avocado who?
Avocado cold!

Knock, Knock
Who's there?
Alma
Alma who?
Alma cookies are gone,
    and I want some more!

Knock, Knock
Who's there?
Dog
Dog who?
Doggone it, open the door.
It's snowing out here!

Knock, Knock
Who's there?
Isabel
Isabel who?
Isabel on your bike?

Knock, Knock
Who's there?
Ferd
Ferd who?
Ferd any good Knock-Knocks lately?

Knock, Knock
Who's there?
Seth
Seth who?
Seth me – And what I seth, goes.

Knock, Knock
Who's there?
O'Shea
O'Shea who?
O'Shea can you shee,
   by the dawn's early light.

Knock, Knock
Who's there?
Leaf
Leaf who?
Please, leaf me alone.

Knock, Knock
Who's there?
Canada
Canada who?
Canada dog come ina da house?

Knock, Knock
Who's there?
Phillip
Phillip who?
Phillip my tank, please.

Knock, Knock
Who's there?
Debris
Debris who?
Debris or not debris, dat is the question.

Knock, Knock
Who's there?
Denny
Denny who?
I don't know. Denny he tell you his name?

Knock, Knock
Who's there?
Gopher
Gopher who?
Gopher a touchdown, rah rah.

Knock, Knock
Who's there?
Otis
Otis who?
Otis a wonderful day
    for a ride in the park.

Knock, Knock
Who's there?
Hugo
Hugo who?
Hugo your way and I'll go mine.

Knock, Knock
Who's there?
Howard
Howard who?
Howard is the ground when you slip on a banana peel.

Knock, Knock
Who's there?
Diesel
Diesel who?
Diesel be your last chance.

Knock, Knock
Who's there?
Ida
Ida who?
If Ida known you were coming,
Ida baked a cake.

Knock, Knock
Who's there?
Fiddlestick
Fiddlestick who?
If your sneakers get holes,
 your fiddlestick out.

Knock, Knock
Who's there?
Banana
Knock, Knock
Who's there?
Banana.
Knock, Knock
Who's there?
Orange
Orange who?
Orange you glad I didn't
 say Banana?

Knock, Knock
Who's there?
Wayne
Wayne who?
Waynedrops keep
 faw-wing on my head.

Knock, Knock
Who's there?
Chesterfield
Chesterfield who?
Chesterfield my leg so I slapped him.

Knock, Knock
Who's there?
Pizza
Pizza who?
Pizza on earth,
    good will to men.

Knock, Knock
Who's there?
Beets
Beets who?
Beets me; I forgot my name.

Knock, Knock
Who's there?
Reed
Reed who?
Reed this book and find out.

Knock, Knock
Who's there?
Freddy
Freddy who?
Freddy or not, here I come.

Knock, Knock
Who's there?
Utah
Utah who?
Utah a putty cat!

Knock, Knock
Who's there?
Victor
Victor who?
Victor his hair out!

Knock, Knock
Who's there?
Rhoda
Rhoda who?
Rhoda horse all the way through Texas.

Knock, Knock
Who's there?
Tuba
Tuba who?
Tuba toothpaste.

Knock, Knock
Who's there?
Shelby
Shelby who?
Shelby comin' round the mountain when she comes . . .

OO-HOO HOO HOO

Knock, Knock
Who's there?
Butter
Butter who?
Butter late than never.

Knock, Knock
Who's there?
Little old lady
Little old lady who?
Oh, I didn't know you could yodel!